7-Figure Onl Agency At 23 Years Old:

Jeremy Haynes

by Ben Gothard,

Founder & CEO of Gothard Enterprises LLC

Author of CEO at 20: A Little Book for Big Dreams

Text and Illustration Copyright © 2017 by Benjamin Pressner Gothard. All rights reserved.

All rights reserved. This book or parts thereof may not be reproduced in any form, stored in any retrieval system, or transmitted in any form by any means — electronic, mechanical, photocopy, recording, or otherwise — without prior written permission of the publisher, except as provided by United States of America copyright law. For permission requests, contact the publisher at:

bgothard@gothardenterprises.com

ISBN-13: 978-1985755673

ISBN-10: 198575567X

Online Marketing Agency

Building a massive online marketing agency is difficult for anybody. Jeremy Haynes took his digital marketing agency to 7-figures in under 12 months at 23 years of age, and he shares the story of how he did it in this interview!

Starting his entrepreneurial journey at a young age, Jeremy had to escape his hometown to find more opportunity when he started making more money than everyone he knew through his first business.

After moving around from place to place, Jeremy has built the largest go-to personality branding digital agency called Megalodon Marketing in Miami, Florida and Beverly Hills, California with in house staff in both locations for all roles within the company.

He's also coached and mentored digital agency owners through his training program the DMM - Digital Marketing Manuscript that he launched after training in Tai Lopez programs; i.e. The SMMA program, The Entrepreneur Start Kit, and How To Be A Traveling CEO along with co-authoring in his new book.

Jeremy has since added over 5,000+ paying mentees into his own coaching product with a credible reputation in the information product industry driving results for not just himself--for his clients too at scale across an array of industries.

He has customers and clients across the globe and regularly acts as a marketing and advertising adviser to celebrity personalities, NY Times Best-Selling Authors, Speakers, Businesses, Ecommerce Companies, and entrepreneurs with the help of the 25+ person team of Megalodon Marketing.

This is the origin story of Jeremy Haynes, and he lays out exactly how he reached extraordinary levels of success in his life at such a young age. His story is a testament to the fact that we can all achieve our dreams through whichever vehicle we decide to pursue them through. You can learn more about turning your dreams into reality by watching more interviews http://www.project.co/ !

This book is a transcription of the interview, unedited. Hopefully you can get as much out of the interview as I did hosting it!

Ben: Good morning everybody. We're here with Jeremy Haynes from Akron, Ohio. Jeremy, you want to introduce yourself?

Jeremy: What's going on everybody? My name is Jeremy. As Ben said, I'm from Akron, Ohio and I currently reside in Miami Beach. I run a personality development company, a digital agency if you will. And I'm talking to my boy Ben today.

Ben: Thanks for that, so let's jump right into it. Question number one: what is your story?

Jeremy: Good question. I was born up in Akron, Ohio. It was a really shady place. It was really negative; it was a really chop at your knees cutthroat environment, meaning the people work there—like my family, my peers' family, everybody—was working in a factory with a really low wage job. People were in thirty to forty thousand a year but they were cool with it. If somebody made 50K, watch out. Can you imagine being raised in that kind of environment?

As an entrepreneur, everybody can relate to the fact that environment is very critical to your success and that was one of my first lessons when I was younger. Nothing made sense to me, and I learned everything the hard way and I learned very quickly that my environment sucked where I was. So I knew I wanted to get out. At sixteen, I started out my first company; it's video production. I started doing music videos for some friends and that led to another friend and that led to somebody I didn't know then somebody else I didn't know; then I started getting paid for it. That led to commercial businesses calling me and it was crazy. I banked $60,000 in three months in Ohio. All of a sudden all my peers, my friends, my parents themselves—everybody, they're trying to tell me I had to go to school and this and that. I was like, guys; I just made more than everybody, you can't tell me what to do. So that was kind of tough for me. I was really low key about it. Honestly, I didn't tell anybody that when I was growing up because I felt like it was a threat. I felt like it was going to be bad if I told people.

Anyway, I knew I needed people skills so I put people in management positions in my video production company and so I took a hit financially because, come time I was seventeen and a half and I was graduating high school— like I said, I knew I needed people skills and real life was about to hit—I got into a sales job, actually. So I was direct TV and in the sales job—you're probably like, well Jeremy, why'd you step down from being an entrepreneur? I really didn't; the company still runs today and I still made money on it. But it wasn't going to be enough to get me out of a while because I didn't have enough resources, I didn't know enough. There were no mentors; there was nobody I could reach out to. I mean, the Internet was popping, but I didn't know about educational online yet. I didn't have the resources that we have today. I felt very hopeless, if you will.

Like I said, I got into the sales job—I was so good at the sales job that they laid out a sheet of 30 cities in front of me and told me I get to pick a city to go to. At the time, Tallahassee was the best looking one. I was going to go there; and all of a sudden Denver popped up. I had family in Colorado Springs about an hour south of Denver. I chose to go out there. Direct TV moved me out to Denver and that was sweet.

But to be a hundred percent transparent, in Denver, I sucked at Direct TV. And Denver was a very intellectual society. It was, to be quite frank, all white people. It was just weird. It wasn't my normal environment and I have 18 years of Ohio condition so I quickly became exposed to the fact that I have to overcome a ton of stuff that was ingrained into me; that I was learning the hard way wasn't the right way to think. I kind of worked into a relationship with the guys in the cellphone kiosk and I ended up transferring positions from Direct TV to the cellphone kiosk.

It's kind of a turning point in the story because this is where I learned more. I made a little more money than I was making—and I was still in sales, right? In Denver, I'll be very transparent once again; weed became legal that year. So everybody and their momma's cousin in Denver was smoking weed. In public—I mean everybody. It was cool, but I wasn't too into it. I mean, I'd smoke occasionally and it really slowed me down to be honest. So that's what I noticed about myself. I've always been very fast and very uppity; very quick with my response time and the way that I like to move and the way that I like to get things done and everybody in Denver was very slow. Very, very slow. In Denver, if you speak this fast, somebody would tell you to stop and slow down and say it again and that they didn't understand you.

It was a beautiful place; beautiful mountains, beautiful city, lot of money being thrown back into the city from all the money they were making from weed. Anyway, I had an old buddy move out from Ohio that he had saved — he was one of the people who couldn't really do shit themselves and so I pulled him out of the trenches and allowed him to live with me out in Colorado. That buddy that came out had gone to Miami for three days and he loved it so much, he decided to tell me that he loved it that much and he wanted me to risk moving down there. In reality, he was so weak that he couldn't move down there himself because he couldn't survive on his own. He's a follower type. He needed my leadership whether he knows that or not. So, we moved to Miami. It was sweet. I moved down here with a $125; sat on a suitcase for a month and a half in my living room. I was on the cusp of overtime — if anybody's familiar with overtime, it's like the shooting ground for first forty-eight, it's rough.

I was still in Costco at the time in the cellphone kiosk—I moved down here to improve my income and move in to the apartment that I was in. I moved down to the Costco position in cellphones when I met a guy and he was in Costco, walking around and I sold him a phone. And he just like who I was so much, he liked my background that he asked me to come into his company and I became his head of marketing. It was sick; I believe I was nineteen at the time — or maybe early twenties — and the gentleman, his name is Peter San, and Peter reached out to me, I guess in Costco, he brought me into his company. He's head of marketing and gave me a ton of stuff. He threw me into a bunch of a stuff that I didn't really know of.

He brought me back into the marketing side of business and got me reconfigured in what I love to do — which was control and manage people's perspectives on how they perceive a product. I was doing that the time through talking to people and kind of manipulating perspective with words; whereas marketing is a passion because of the challenge. How can I get in front of somebody digitally to manage their perspective and have them take an action without them realizing that they're being pushed into that situation for marketing tactics and skill that I was laying down. So that was really fun, it's the moral of the story.

There came a time where I put my resume out there. So then my gut just told me I needed to pull my resume out. So I did, and I get a call from this recruiter and it's a recruiter for Grant Cardone. I never heard of Grant—I didn't know who he was, didn't know what he was about—and they said that they needed an email marketing manager and somebody to manage his Infusionsoft account for them and they had no idea how to use it. Anyway, that could be a long story short but what happened is that the guy who brought me into his company as the head of marketing comes to me the next day. So I put my resume up, I get a call from a recruiter, and then the next day, my boss comes in—the guy who hired me for the head of marketing—he's like, you know Jeremy, I unfortunately got to distribute my company. I'm selling it off and there's not going to be a position for you, the company is just buying us for the assets and not buying us for the structure. So that being said, I got to let you go but you got three days. I'm like, okay. So I just call the recruiter back up. I'm like, 'hey, good news.' They're like, 'sweet, you can start on Monday?' I was like, 'well I mean I'd like to interview there but yeah, I guess.' I walk into this guy's office that I never heard of — I Googled him before I showed up — so I Googled Grant Cardone and see how big he is. I see what he's up to and I see who he really is and I Googled Grant Cardone network — and I see a hundred million dollars. I was like, 'oh shit, okay.' So I go in for an interview the following Monday; got fired on Friday, got an interview in Grant's office in Monday and I could keep this really light. I sit down in the interview with him and I got the job and that was cool but when I go in the interview, the interesting part of his office is—it's a beautiful office. It's very modern, straight down the road here in Miami. Anyway, when I sit down this old dude sitting across from me in the lobby and I don't know who he is. He's got a really nice looking suit, looked European, and very old but not old enough to not have life in him; he's very energetic. I come to find out this was a fifty billion dollar man; his name's Daniel Peña and I was just conversating with him for ten, fifteen minutes before my interview. He didn't tell me who he was; I didn't know who he was until I came back to fill my position in Grant's company three or four days later after I secured the position and I was watching him on Power Players—which is a show where you create interviews with people like that. Anyway, long story short, come into Grant's office, I'm an email marketing manager—so I manage 150,000 people in the

CRM, which is Customer Relation Management system, and train 25 sales people in Grant's office for their sales team—because they're all using this system and had no clue how to use it. I got in the position where I realize there was no marketing. I got nothing, dude. We might all know Grant on his podcast and his interview but what you got to understand is Grant is pretty sales-y. Grant knows how to push but he doesn't know how to pull. I say that lightly because people are attracted to him and people do get pulled into what he does but that's from these different systems that are in place now that—let's say you hit a landing page and you leave, you're going to be pulled back because there'll be Facebook ads that are dynamically put in front of you based on the fact that you just hit a certain product page and didn't buy it—but you have bought something else. There'll be Google display targeting ads that will be put in front of you on 86% of the web pages that are based on what you're going to buy and if you hit a page and you do buy, then now's the time to buy something else. Or if we have your email already collected and you get on one of our sites and you leave, you get an email follow up right away. All these things that he wasn't doing that were the little things in marketing that a marketer or an advertiser will know of that make a ton of money. So I sat back, just having done all that being head of marketing for a company, now stepping down in a sense just to email marketing and my intention was to step back up. By the time I left that office, there was 453,000 people in the database through not purchasing lists—with purchase list and with list that they'd gotten, they were at about 560,000. So stepped in the door, 150,000 people in a day, left with 453,000. Stepped in the door,

$40,000 a month coming in, left with an average of $1.8 million a month coming in just through e-commerce. Stepped in, 25 different sales people had no clue how to use Infusionsoft, I left about maybe a third of them, if I'm being honest, were fluent in Infusionsoft and those are the people who are the core sales, people who didn't rotate in and out. I became self-aware of my skill, I became self-aware with everything I was doing which was everything digital. Email marketing, Facebook ads, Google display ads, LinkedIn ads, and we do some Twitter ads occasionally. I would help orient the landing pages so I would draw the landing pages on this big whiteboard walls that we had and then two graphic guys would execute all the assets we need to build the page and we had two web developers that would go build the site itself and I would go market to shit out of it. Eventually, we had a digital properties manager come in and kind of manage us collectively since why we had no leadership and since we're making so much money at a certain point — or to be quite frank, it's very hard for me to make somebody $1.8 to $2.5 million a month off of a product that I saw developed. It was just video courses. It was just a man standing in front of a video camera and articulating the knowledge that you held from the experience that you gained and people were paying a thousand dollars for one year of access to these different videos. I saw people buy a $49 web ticket where we made $800,000 off of on one event. It's nuts, it's just videos. That's it.

Ben: That's incredible.

Jeremy: The videos will be turned into audio docs and those would sell for $10 on the low for an mp3 of a book to a high end of $250 for an audio file for one of these three and a half hour webinars. I was the driving force behind training the entire sales team and educating the sales team on where and how they communicate with other people on different parts of the sales teams. I created dynamic email follow up that would cater messages to people based on where they were on the sales process.

I was dishing out maybe $50,000 to $100,000 a month in advertising spend making back a four to one return on the lowest. In other days, I came in and tracked ROI and we would have a twelve to one return. That's a 1200% return on our investment. You put a dollar in the system, you get $10 to $12 dollars back in some cases. It was sick, but I was only getting paid like ten to about sixteen thousand in a month one time. They just kind of jerked around on bonuses and just like any business they want to retain as much financial intake as they can. It kind of became unethical to a certain point. I don't need to trash any names or go any further on that but there just came a point where I didn't agree with our current pay structure, from how it was manipulated in certain cases when we didn't meet a particular work standard on how and what we were doing to acquire said finances. It wasn't very fair to us.

That being said, I made it fair to me and I stepped out of my position. I started my digital agency and Grant thankfully supports me. He can't go against me in a sense because he preaches entrepreneurship and it'd be very critical for him to go against what it is that I've chosen to do. Most of the people in the internal aspect of the company agree with what I've done and see where I've gone and who I've become and the reason why I did what I did.

I needed to help more people dude. I was making somebody $1.8 million a month with the help of a digital team and I recreated the digital team. One of two graphic designers for Grant who was fired over not tweeting one of the tweets that an advertiser was paying us to tweet for him got let go, so I hired him immediately. He's my creative director. He ran all of Grant's social mediums, did everything but Grant's videos which obviously he couldn't do, and he's my creative director so he does all my graphics, he runs all my social development for all my clients that we have on board. I'm the advertising director so I take everything that I already did in Grant's office and I scaled it down to a point where I can do it for several people, monitor everything, and put people in positions where they make millions of dollars a month. In most cases hundreds of thousands, or in most common cases tens of thousands dollars a month from taking them as a personality, developing a monetization model around it—meaning creating websites, funnels, email follow up, marketing automation to take those leads and shoot them to the different digital mediums to target them in real time. I literally recreated the omnipresent advertising models for each one of my personality grand clients.

I drive a lot of revenue sales and leads into these personalities businesses. One other asset that I have in my company is one of the sales people for Grant, her name's Sheila, and Sheila's my VP of sales and Sheila is in a position where she looks over my internal communications — so she communicates to all my clients internally and her responsibility is to bring people to the external part of the world, which is everybody, into our organization. Her responsibility is sales of course and communication management.

She's an incredible woman and she does an incredible job and I'm really excited to continue developing her role as we go here. That's my core in my company and I bust five other people out on payroll; senior copywriters, video production. I went from about $100,000 a year, or maybe like it's probably around $110,000 or $120,000 with some of the other things I was doing outside the office — to now, I don't really like to track my personal income but if I had to gauge it I would probably say it's upwards of $250,000 to $260,000 this year but I invested all of it into my business. My business would clear about $900,000 in the first year of operation and I was told by Grant on his show, the Cardone Zone, the day after I left that I was going to bail in four months. You know how that goes.

Ben: Right, right.

Jeremy: But yes, I went from Ohio just getting thrown a ton of negative criticism every day of my life on what I could and couldn't do and blew the factory workers out of the water and moved to Denver and after living in Denver and things got slow I got pulled down in Miami and became a head of marketing out of nowhere, got into Grant's office, became the digital marketing specialist and was banking a per salary grade of a couple million a month, and now I do it for everybody else.

Ben: That's incredible. You kind of talk a lot about your past and your history and how you got to where you are. But moving forward, what is the one most important thing that you want to accomplish in your lifetime?

Jeremy: Our mission is to drive $8 billion in gross revenue by helping our clients help people in ethical digital monetization model. So check this out; I was in Ohio and I had nobody, right? One of the highlights of that story was that Tony Robins, when I was seventeen years old, popped up on the right hand side of the YouTube suggested video column, and I watched a video called How to Build Self-Confidence by Tony Robins. And I would never forget that moment. I was surrounded by people who had the shittiest mentalities, were very negative, who in no way shape or form knew how I grew into the people I wanted to grow into. And out of nowhere this Tony Robins guy comes in as a support system and tells me that I can do it. He teaches me how to do it and gives me actionable tips that I can apply to my life. I'll never forget that moment. It felt like the help that I needed; I was in a cornered environment where everybody was cutthroat chop at your knees negative, and there was that one person that helped me get out of that position just by educating me through the Internet.

It changed my life and then I randomly ended up in Grant's office where I helped a man take a message and spread it to the masses. We would get testimonials back that would literally say that they changed their own lives just through this online education. That's what I love to see. Every single day, I wake up and do what I do, Ben, because I know that there's people in the world who are trapped in that corner, who have no help, who have no support, who have no system or structure, and need help. The people that I work with—I work with the most incredible people that you could ever meet in your life; that if you spoke to would change your life in a conversation.

To be quite frank, I almost choke up just talking about it because I know that the message that I spread to the masses for each one of my clients helps so many people. I see the testimonials; I love being the driving force behind messages like that. But I have a bigger sense of thinking now, right? So knowing what I just said, now you got to think the big picture, okay? Uber right now, if Uber bought a fleet of autonomous vehicles right now — like overnight, boom, they just bought them — 140,000 jobs for Uber drivers just got wiped out. Unemployment just went from 18% to 33% overnight; that would reverberate into a ton of different industries. But without going into all of that, what would immediately happen is 140,000 different individuals would go from a low skill set of just driving a car—they're like a robotic position, if you will—anything that can be automated, or become autonomous, is not a skill that humans need to be doing. That's why automation is occurring; it's supposed to make our lives easier. But what it really does is it reconditions the people that are in those lower skill set positions to have to specialize their skill or get wiped out. And it's as easy as that.

I tied this into what I'm talking about in spreading the messages because there's about to be some shit that goes down in the world. There's going to be some big change coming really quick and if 140,000 people get wiped out of the market, I know that with my clients' information that I have that everything that relates to online education—and just imagine how desperate these individuals will become when they have to specialize their skill sets almost overnight just to survive, or just to pay for the roof above their heads. Just to feed their family members, they have to become better.

And to become better, you need education. To have education, you have to have essentially the resource to find it which everybody does now, which is the internet. My mission is when all these industries get disrupted and all of these people become unemployed and all of these people have to turn to how they can become better, I'm really excited to be a resource and a source of that information because there had been millions of lives that are changed drastically. The people that have incredible skills will have to get them. People who don't have skills will have to acquire skills. The people who get wiped out on those markets will either transition into something else or they'll just become depressed and give up on life.

I have clients that can cater each one of those niches for every bit of information that you would need to grow into or grow better or grow out of it. I'm really excited of what's to come because that's going to recondition the world and we're going to see a more competent, more skilled version of humans that we currently know and understand. Just imagine all those robotic humans right now. All the people that are walking dead are not necessarily be in positions where they're confident themselves or might not be thinking every day. Can you imagine if every single person in the world thought? Like I'm talking about people that wake up and say 'oh I need breakfast.' I'm talking about the people who are forced into a corner who have to think of ways out. You know that thinking. Not a lot of people choose to think like that. There's going to be a time very quickly where everybody's thinking like that at once. I don't know what's going to happen but I'm excited to see it. I'm excited to be the helping hand on the other side that's helping pull people up.

Ben: You're saying a lot about you want to be the helping hand to help people up. Well it seems like you had a lot of people that kind of helped you along the way, whether it be Peter, Daniel, and Tony Robins. Who do you think would be the biggest mentors in your life?

Jeremy: To be quite frank, from afar, I would 100% say Tony Robins. He has so much online information that I could look up anything that I wanted to look up with Tony and he's going to have an answer for me on something that could give me a spark or a push or the action that which helped pull me up from wherever I'm at that position. Up close, no doubt, Grant Cardone. When I walked into that office, my thinking—keep in mind, still to this day I find random things in my thought process that were conditioned into me from Ohio or from that low-level mentality and I always, always step out of my way to recondition myself and I find those things. Through Grant, every single day I learn something new. Massive action, communication in high frequency—I could go on and on about the different business lessons I learned from him first-hand. Even when he wouldn't speak, just being observant in his office, there's a very strong set of lessons that you could pull every single day. It's an incredible environment, honestly. So Grant and Tony for sure.

Ben: Okay and I have two more questions for you. The first one is: if you could pass on one piece of advice, what would it be?

Jeremy: I would tell you to sprint your ass up, because every day I freak out because I feel like I don't have enough time. I feel from the amount of work that I need to do and the level in which I need to operate on after I reconditioned my thinking to be so big that there's not enough time. Managing your time is the greatest asset but a lot of people are really slow and a lot of people act like tomorrow's the day to do things that should be done today. A lot of people don't try to maximize and really squeeze in everything that they can do. So one word, it'd be sprint.

Ben: Wow. And then I guess the last question would be: is there anything about yourself that I did not ask you about in this interview that you like to share?

Jeremy: Yeah, I have a really good piece of advice; I'm 22 and I'm stepping into a position where I will manage a million dollar a year business probably a year and one month after my initial operation started and it's not overwhelming. It's not something that feels out of my reach, it's not something that feels like I can't manage but one of the greatest lessons that I ever learned in life besides having to sprint for the finish—that I'd like to repeat here—because I feel like you have a very entrepreneurial audience of course, and they're going to appreciate this.

Speed is power but power is nothing without control. And no matter where you're at, no matter what level you're on, no matter how fast you feel you're moving, power is nothing without control. You really have to understand that, you really have to apply it to your life because you could obviously relate it to several metaphors like if I go from driving a Toyota Camry and then I step into a Lamborghini — speed is power, I'm going to feel that, but the power is nothing without control, and as an unexperienced driver coming from a very low-end vehicle comparably to a Lamborghini, I'm not going to be able to control the vehicle but I'll have the speed of the vehicle and a lot of people misconstrue that. A lot of people get into Lamborghinis without being able to control them. A lot of people don't try to work themselves up to be able to manage the power that they're getting and that's one of my greatest assets that I could give anybody in life is, you always have to educate and train yourself every single day. You need to look at yourself as a pro-athlete. You need to look at yourself like what are you doing to better yourself in every area of who you are today to allow you to drive your Lamborghini as fast as you want because power is nothing without control.

Ben: That's fantastic. Alright Jeremy, well thank you very much for tuning in today and thank you to everybody who's listening. I hope you guys could learn something from Jeremy; he has a really great story. So this is Jeremy Haynes from Akron, Ohio. Thank you very much.

Jeremy: Appreciate it, Ben.

Made in the USA
Coppell, TX
04 October 2020